Grief Letters

Devotions to Help Navigate the Loss of a Loved One

D1306069

Karen Bransgrove

WESTBOW·
PRESS
A DIVISION OF THOMAS NELSON
& ZONDERVAN

WestBow Press books may be ordered through booksellers or by contacting:

WestBow Press
A Division of Thomas Nelson & Zondervan
1663 Liberty Drive
Bloomington, IN 47403
www.westbowpress.com
1 (866) 928-1240

ISBN: 978-1-4908-6966-7 (sc)
ISBN: 978-1-4908-6967-4 (hc)
ISBN: 978-1-4908-6965-0 (e)

Library of Congress Control Number: 2015902144

Print information available on the last page.

WestBow Press rev. date: 3/16/2015

Contents

Acknowledgements

To my sons, Austin and Chris: I am so very proud of the way you have both handled your grief journeys. Thank you for your constant support, encouragement, and love. You are a blessing to me. Your daddy would be pleased with the way you have chosen to live your lives. My prayer is that you will continue to honor your Heavenly Father.

To my family: I hear people talk about the dysfunctional families they endure. I realize the gift I have in all of you. While we are not perfect, may not always agree on things, and cannot talk regularly, I am certain of your love and support. Thank you.

To my friends: Thank you for sticking by me through the many tears and lapses of memory you witnessed as I learned to deal with my grief. I am grateful that you chose to remain part of my life. I realize it has not always been easy for you. This journey has brought me new friends as well, and my life is richer because of you. For those of you who read an earlier version of my story, your encouragement helped me move forward with courage to create *Grief Letters*.

To my editor, Isabelle Szucs: Thank you for taking on *Grief Letters* as your first project. I will always be grateful for the patience and grace you gave, waiting for my tears to stop flowing before we would get back to work, chapter by chapter. You allowed me to keep the integrity of what I desired to share.

Introduction

Dear One,

    If you had told me twenty-six months ago that I would be starting a book about my journey with grief, I would have said, "Impossible!" But in the last three years, I have seen God do a lot of impossible things. I have discovered great comfort in the promise "I can do all things through Him who gives me strength." (Philippians 4:13 New International Version) While there have been many people who have encouraged me and walked this difficult journey with me, the 'Him' in the Scripture above is God Almighty and He is my absolute source of strength, hope, survival, and joy. God never faces anything that He cannot handle. Impossible is not in His vocabulary. I find peace in realizing His faithfulness and great comfort in His promise to always be with me.

    I am writing this book to share that very promise with you. I sincerely hope that in reading *Grief Letters*, you come to know this God of whom I write. He knows you intimately and desires for you to get better acquainted with Him. My prayer is that you will not be the same person finishing this book as you are beginning it. May you be blessed as you read, learn, and process through your journey of grief.

Your fellow journeyer,

Karen

CHAPTER 1

And Suddenly Life Changed

Dear One,

It was a day like any other. I left home that morning to go to work, kissed Alan good-bye and wished him a good day. He had a job interview but was not feeling well. Flu symptoms had been hitting him for a couple of days and he just could not seem to shake the illness. Little did I know that when I would return to the house eight hours later my world would never again be the same.

Alan called me that afternoon and said that he still felt bad and had even canceled the interview. I told him my meetings were finished and I was headed home. I suggested that perhaps we should go to the hospital and have him examined. He told me he wanted to wait until the morning to see how he was feeling.

On the way home, I called him back multiple times as my concern increased, but he did not answer. As I drove into the neighborhood, I vividly recall feeling certain that something had happened. Not wanting to believe it, I actually spoke out loud to God in the car. "Are you trying to tell me he is dead?" I felt God's arms around me as I drove into the driveway and ran into the house.

The next seven hours were ones I still do not care to recall or relive. What I do want to remember is that God placed special people in my life that evening. The EMT first responders arrived and did their best while the police officer sat at the dining-room table with me, trying to keep me occupied and out of the bedroom. Later, my neighbor came over and took care of the house for me while I went to the hospital.

Both my senior pastor and associate pastor were already waiting for me at the emergency room. My good friend and teammate from work arrived shortly afterward, joining us in a room tucked far away from the frantic activity that occurs when doctors fight for a person's life. One of our close friends soon came and began taking over for me, making all the necessary arrangements that would consume my life the next four days.

Incredible friends drove up and met our youngest son at the college an hour and a half away and brought him home to me that night. My church purchased a plane ticket to get our oldest son home by the next day as he lived out of state. Another friend spent the night with me, even coming into my bedroom and holding me when I awoke and cried in the middle of the night.

My large and extended family made arrangements to come for the service. My best friend dropped everything and spent the next two weeks with me. She helped with anything I needed and provided many things I had no idea I needed. Numerous church members came in and out of my home that week and silently served me by cooking, cleaning, and praying.

Looking back now, I realize God met my needs. He was there in the form of friends and family. I truly believe God uses people to minister to His children, especially in the midst of pain and suffering. I am blessed that my friends were Godly, wise people who did well by me.

In the Bible, we read how Job also suffered great loss. However, his friends did not understand the ways of God. They actually blamed Job for his misfortunes and encouraged him to curse God for the bad things that were happening. I am grateful that instead of telling me I was to blame for Alan's death and that God was obviously my enemy, my friends supported me through countless, selfless acts of kindness.

There are times the grief and tears still wash over me, though not every day. I have moments when I weep with such abandon you would think these emotions were brand new and that everything had happened yesterday. Scripture tells us that the Lord "will wipe away the tears from all faces." (Isaiah 25:8 NIV). Therefore, I believe my sadness and tears are important to God and a vital part of my grief journey.

As you open up and release your pain by being sad, allowing yourself to cry, and perhaps shouting and venting out loud a bit, God will soothe you. He hears your cry. He knows your pain. God's beloved son, Jesus Christ, died so that you and I can have the hope and assurance of once again seeing our loved ones. That reunion in Heaven is only possible if you know Jesus. Not just know about Jesus, but really *know* Him.

As we walk through this book together, my desire is for you to see Jesus through my grief journey and be able to look for Him in yours. Hold fast, Dear One; you are not abandoned. Even when your world has suddenly changed and turned upside down, you do not have to be alone.

I am proud of you for beginning this journey of walking through your grief. Read on and may you find strength for the days ahead by leaning on the One who is strong enough to carry you.

At the end of each short chapter, I have listed a few application exercises to assist you in your journey of grief. I found these exercises helpful and I hope you can use them as well. Take your time and work at your own pace.

Your fellow journeyer,
Karen

Application:

- ➢ Look for ways that God has been with you. Have you been able to see or feel His presence? If so, compile a list to refer to later. Seeing that evidence written down can make it more real and can remind you of the truth that God is indeed in your life and is concerned for you.
- ➢ Who were the people that have helped you most in this difficult time? Did God show Himself through them or through a special moment or event?
- ➢ Perhaps you need to take some time and ask yourself, "What is my relationship with God?" Do you remember a time in your life that you prayed and asked Jesus to forgive your sin? He died on the cross for you and without Him, you remain separated from God, living life on your own.

If you do not have this personal relationship and would like to know more about it, then turn to the back of this book and read about God's love for you in the "Meeting Jesus" chapter. He cares for you and wants you as His own, Dear One. Knowing Jesus personally has been instrumental in allowing me to heal and move forward in life.

CHAPTER 2

How Much Are My Tears Worth?

Dear One,

What are tears? Science tells us:

> You may only think of tears as those salty drops that fall from your eyes when you cry. Actually, your tears clean your eyes every time you blink. Tears also keep your eyes moist, which is important for your vision.[1]

I love the fact that tears clean our eyes and I believe God has used them to cleanse me these past few years. When I have cried, my tears became a cleansing agent that allowed pent-up pain and hurt to temporarily be washed away. After a good cry, I would feel exhausted, but somehow relieved. The kind of crying I am describing is not dainty and quaint. The tearful episodes I write of are painful, ugly, and consuming. This type of weeping takes your breath away, quickly turns your face red, wet, and hot, and is accompanied by uncontrollable sobbing that wracks the body with movement. You could say I have become an expert at letting the tears flow.

I soon realized there was no holding back from experiencing these occurrences and I could not be refined or calm during them. Try as I might, it was impossible to honor some of the wishes of those around me. There were people who were uncomfortable with my crying and would express, "Oh don't cry. You'll make me cry." While I now understand they failed to know what to say, fulfilling their request was not really possible. There were times I felt the tears coming for seemingly no reason and with little warning. I could not stop them even when I attempted to, so I simply stopped trying. Not wishing for others to feel awkward, I quickly learned to excuse myself and find a private place in which to shed my tears.

One of the best gifts I have ever received from people was the permission and freedom to express myself. They did not squirm or look away. Instead, they stayed near, remained silent, and graciously accepted my display of emotion. This freedom was exactly what I needed to be lifted from the huge, dark hole of grief.

Tears are God's gift for many reasons. Cleansing and moistening our eyes is just the most obvious one. An even better tear-related gift is realizing that God brings us relief through crying in the midst of our fear, pain, and suffering. Praise God for tears! Luke 11:35 states that even Jesus wept. This may be the shortest verse in the Bible, yet it is a power-packed one. Jesus knew pain and sorrow, just as you and I do. His beloved friend, Lazarus, had died and it hurt Him to see the sisters, Mary and Martha, crying and distressed. Jesus knew what was going to happen and that He was going to bring Lazarus back to life.

Nevertheless, He cried and acknowledged His own pain and grief in the midst of loss – even temporary loss.

Teaching others about grief is another gift that comes from letting our tears flow. I believe the people that have walked closely with me these past few years cannot help but be changed a bit because of what they have experienced with me. Learning to cry and be comfortable with tears is not a skill everyone possesses. Therefore, I believe it is something from which everyone can benefit. Living with tears, either your own or someone else's, is a worthwhile skill to develop.

Dear One, Jesus knows our pain. He experienced loss and felt grief. Because He faced all those emotions, He is capable of bringing us to the other side of our own grief. Do not be ashamed of your tears. You do not need to apologize for them. Even though I may still say, "I'm sorry" at times when I cry in front of someone, I am not sorry to shed tears throughout this journey. I want people to understand that I am not asking for pity. Instead, I am allowing myself the right to grieve since that is the only way to travel this difficult road successfully. It really does not benefit us to detour around grief – we must go through it to make it to the other side.

Let God dry your tears as they fall. May you know His love and compassion in the midst of your damp, tear-filled journey. Experience His cleansing power through your tears.

Your fellow journeyer,

Karen

Application:

> ➤ Do you notice things that make you cry? For instance, are you more tearful when stressed about finances and bills? Perhaps preparing to travel places is harder for you now. Discovering your reasons for crying will allow you to have grace with yourself when you feel the tears coming and will help prepare you to better deal with the situation instigating those tears. Begin to make a list so that you can see a pattern and become better equipped to handle these times to keep from being surprised.

> ➤ Look back over your journey since your loss. Can you identify the progress you are making with your tears? Are you crying less? If not, do not be too hard on yourself. We all grieve and move forward at different paces.

> ➤ If you find yourself feeling hopeless or depressed for a long period of time and unable to eat or care for yourself, please seek the assistance of a doctor. There is no shame in getting professional help for this very real challenge in your life.

CHAPTER 3

Why Do "Bad" Things Happen?

Dear One,

I want to assure you that no matter what it is that you are now facing, what you have dealt with in your past, or what your future may hold, God is Sovereign. If He is so in control of things, then why do bad things happen to good people? After asking myself that question numerous times these past three years, I would like to share some of my conclusions with you.

First of all, even though we may not consider ourselves bad people, none of us are truly good. When we are willing to be compared to the standard of God, we have to admit the truth that at times, we fail. "There is no one righteous, not even one; there is no one who understands, no one who seeks God. All have turned away, they have together become worthless; there is no one who does good, not even one." (Romans 3:10–12 NIV)

The Bible explains that each of us is born a sinner; selfish by nature and required to surrender to God in order to see any good in us or produce anything worthwhile through us. It is only by God's grace that we experience any worth at all. What we deserve for our failures, our sin, is punishment. When we are willing to admit to that fact, why then, do we question God when life is not always good? Fortunately, the penalty we deserve is not what we actually receive because of God's grace and forgiveness that is provided through Jesus Christ.

How do I then explain the difficult times if God is so forgiving and loving? 2 Corinthians 1:18–22 teaches that God desires to give us good things. He wants to say, "Yes!" to His children. We can trust that God is faithful and loving in dealing with His people. The times that we do not hear a "Yes!" from God may mean that "No" is a better answer for our situation even though it makes no sense to us. His "No" is not meant to be cruel, but is a way for Him to teach us what is best. He guides us to wait and trust in His perfect timing. As you learn more about God, you will find it easier to trust and wait upon Him through the pain and sadness of your loss.

There have been times these past years where I have been very conscious of people watching me and measuring God through my display of emotions and reactions to life's events. While this has been a heavy and sometimes scary responsibility, it has also forced me to re-evaluate what I believe and know about God. He alone is trustworthy. Everyone else may leave me, but I trust beyond the shadow of a doubt that He will always be by my side and has a plan for my life.

Realizing that the God of the universe is personally acquainted with me and chooses to use me in pointing others to see His glory through my grief journey is humbling. Yet I believe that is exactly what He is doing with my life.

I am no one special. He wants to be with you as well, Dear One. We have a chance to make God famous and to give Him glory! What an incredible privilege and opportunity.

You may be asking, "What is God's glory and why I am concerned with Him receiving it?" God is the only one who deserves to get credit for anything and everything. "You are worthy, our Lord and God, to receive glory and honor and power, for you created all things, and by your will they were created and have their being." (Rev. 4:11 NIV)

In case you may be thinking that God seems egotistical and selfish expecting all the glory, please read on. I hope you will change your opinion of God as you continue to read this book and learn more of His character.

One of my fondest memories of Alan comes from our first month of marriage. He was still a student in graduate school studying for his Juris Doctorate and I was working hard to support us and pay for school. We sat down together to go through the bills as a married couple for the first time.

He was well acquainted with budgeting and finances as he had already been on his own for several years. However, I knew nothing about this part of life since I lived with my parents until our marriage. After writing checks and subtracting the dollar amounts to come up with a very small balance left in the bank, I was dismayed. Looking at him I said, "But that is not fair. We have the whole month left and hardly any money!" His response was, "Honey, who ever told you life was fair?"

So when you feel that life just is not fair and you find yourself asking, "Why do bad things happen to me?" try to remember that life is not always fair but you are not walking that road alone.

When you hold on long enough to the hand of the Savior, you will reach the other side of your sadness and grief.

Have I arrived at the end of my journey? Do I always see the blessing in spite of my circumstances? Am I excited about the direction my life has taken? No, not always. There are days when I get glimpses of what God may be doing, but then at other times, I still face great uncertainty. I can tell you though, Dear One, that I am doing my best to hold tightly to the very One who will teach me, mold me, and shape me into the woman He intends for me to be.

My hope and goal in surviving His workmanship is to bring Him the glory He alone deserves. I encourage you to join me in that choice of holding on to Him. Do not loosen your grip to give up and let go. He is there to carry you through the really hard, "bad" days so you will see the goodness, happiness, and blessing in your future.

Your fellow journeyer,
Karen

Application:

➤ What is your biggest challenge right now? Spend some time praying and asking God to help you through it. Perhaps writing out your prayers will help you realize what it is that you really need today. Use colorful note cards or poster paper to remind you that His workmanship in your life will be beautiful.

➤ Try hard to find a "Yes" that God has granted you. What blessings do you currently see in your life? If you are having trouble identifying one, perhaps you have a trusted friend who can give you some perspective and point out a way they see God working in your life. Be sure to write these blessings down as you discover them. Looking back will give you hope on those darker, "bad" days that you encounter.

➢ As you begin each day, try to find one good thing upon which to focus. Reviewing your journaling can help. Remember how precious you are to God and that He truly is with you on your grief journey. No one needs to travel this road alone.

CHAPTER 4

Holiday Help

Dear One,

Holidays! Those days that we once greatly anticipated for the joy and fun they provided can now bring anxiety because they are painful reminders that our life has changed. Between Thanksgiving and New Year's I face a number of difficult days: Thanksgiving, the anniversary of Alan's death, his birthday, Christmas Day, and then my birthday. Dealing with holidays can be hard for each of us who have lost a loved one because they are destined to be different.

I experienced the loss of my husband just four short days after Thanksgiving. My sons and I had managed to make it through the funeral and the required traveling to the out-of-state graveside. By the time Christmas rolled around, I was still in shock and had no desire to celebrate anything. We had talked about our options and had every intention of just staying home and not celebrating Christmas that year. I admit I felt guilty doing this. Even though the boys were older, it seemed I was somehow letting them down. Perhaps by not doing anything at all we would be emphasizing our loss even more.

A phone call on Christmas Eve offered a solution. My boss, our ministry pastor, called and invited us to Christmas dinner at their place. On the spur of the moment, I accepted. The boys graciously went along with the plan and the next day we found ourselves seated at their dining-room table. I will forever be grateful for the courage that dear family had to invite three numb, hurting, and socially inept people to their house that day.

Awkward does not even begin to describe those few hours as I sat there feeling uncomfortable and scared. Somehow I felt I was betraying my grief and my husband by attempting to acknowledge the holiday. Even though this way of thinking makes no sense, it does show that in the midst of grief, we are often unable to think logically.

I cannot tell you what we ate that day or exactly what we talked about. Our hosts were gracious and smoothly continued their conversations as I cried periodically throughout the meal. These wise parents must have had quite a talk instructing their pre-teen kids because they were remarkable and seemed quite at ease with us. We did not stay long following the meal, as I was anxious to go home. The continuous effort of trying to reign in my emotions had exhausted me.

As the years have passed, I have managed to learn a few things about holidays. First and foremost, I have given myself permission to totally change the familiar routines. We have not celebrated any major holiday as we did before Alan's death. Not everyone will have this flexibility, freedom, or desire. Sometimes you will want to treasure and hang on to those memories and traditions. However, keeping old customs just did not work for me. I needed new and fresh because the old and familiar hurt too much.

Thanksgiving and Christmas have been spent outside of our home since Alan's passing. We have traveled, gone to friends, rented a condo in the mountains – whatever we felt comfortable with in finding a way to celebrate together. I learned that the actual process of how we spent the day did not matter nearly as much as the fact that we were together with family and friends.

Decorating the house the first two Christmas seasons was too difficult and painful for me. While I was finally able to set up a tree this past Christmas, it was a different one. The ornaments I used were new, as I was not able to dig through our boxes yet and see the treasures we had collected throughout our twenty-six years of marriage. Those are tucked away safely in the closet and ready for use when I gain the courage and strength to open those boxes.

Other special days in the year have been difficult: his birthday, Valentine's Day, my birthday, and our wedding anniversary. Each of those holidays holds a challenge. Navigating difficult days is a learned skill. Being aware that special days tend to bring more sorrow, confusion, anxiety, and stress is imperative in surviving and eventually enjoying those days. My emotions tend to be raw as these days approach. I have decided that is okay. Those feelings are part of the grief journey and need to be dealt with and acknowledged, not ignored and pushed aside or buried deep within.

Comfort and encouragement can be found in a Bible verse that addresses time and change. "There is a time for everything, and a season for every activity under Heaven." (Eccl. 3:1 NIV) The next verses in that chapter list those specifically; "a time to be born and a time to die, a time to plant and a time to uproot, a time to kill and a time to heal, a time to tear down and a time to build, a time to weep and a time to laugh, a time to mourn and a time to dance."" (Eccl. 3:2–4 NIV) We need to give ourselves permission to stop, feel, change, and even stay the same. What works for one person will not necessarily be successful for another.

I am not saying that we should do whatever we want or whatever feels good. We need to be careful and mindful that a life not centered on God is one without purpose and meaning. The way in which we handle our tough days, especially holidays, should be determined by how we sense God guiding us. For those times we are too numb to feel, we must allow godly people in our lives to direct us. God's Word is also a great source in helping us to maneuver difficult times. As you read and make decisions, you can trust He will never guide you to do anything that is not consistent with His Word.

I found great help and encouragement by attending Hope for the Holidays, which is a Grief Share program. This class assists the grieving in "surviving" and hopefully learning to thrive once again through difficult, special days. You can find Grief Share organizations in your area by going to their website for locations. www.griefshare.org [2]

My prayer for you, Dear One, is that you will once again learn to smile and enjoy the holidays without feeling guilt or pain. I know my Alan would want me to laugh and appreciate these special times of the year again. This may currently seem an unattainable goal, though it is possible. You will learn to move from dreading and sorrow to anticipation and laughter. Holidays are guaranteed to be reoccurring events in life. The decision of how to face them is up to you and can be a benefit for years to come.

Your fellow journeyer,

Karen

Application:

> ➤ List the holidays or special days that tend to be the most difficult for you.
>
> ➤ Try to determine if there is a way to change how you think about and plan for those days so that the anxiety and dread of them lessen. For example, I try to not be home alone on the anniversary of Alan's passing.
>
> ➤ Dream a little and think of a goal you can set that will enable you to actually look forward to a holiday. This past Christmas, I rented a condo and we spent family time together in the mountains snowmobiling. This was an activity we had never done before but had always wanted to do. Your dreams do not have to cost a lot of money though. Perhaps you attend a Christmas concert at a local church or bless others by going Christmas caroling in your neighborhood. Christmas lights are always fun to tour. Go find a great location near you and enjoy the sights and sounds of Christmas.
>
> ➤ Pray and ask God to show you how to achieve your new goal. Allow Him to guide your journey.

CHAPTER 5

God's Timing is Always Best

Dear One,

Control. Human nature tempts us to hold on tightly to our schedules, wishes, dreams, and desires, as well as the people we love. I hear families talk of what they have planned for the next ten years. They smile as they explain how they will meet their goals to achieve the future they envision. I understand that.

We spent wonderful years as a family. Enjoying our kids and watching them grow to be incredible godly, young men was a pleasure. Then Alan was laid off, which was not what we had planned at all. While many details could be shared about this situation, let me just say we were suddenly dealing with incredible stress. I believe this situation coupled with several other complications in our lives took a toll on him, causing him to die at an early age.

I do not understand why this happened just as we were entering our "empty nest years" – years in which couples enjoy getting reacquainted. We were looking forward to spending some special time together. We had talked about taking a cruise for our thirtieth wedding anniversary only a few years away. None of that was to be. God had other plans. I see now that those plans also included taking care of my family as we were left behind.

As friends and I dug through the various papers and files in the house the day after Alan passed away, we saw that because of Alan's jobless situation, he was within thirty days of losing a life insurance policy provided through his former employer. This particular detail did not sink in until weeks later. It is now evident that God used that insurance annuity to help provide for my future and finish paying for our youngest son's college. I am not saying that God had caused Alan's death to care of us. God can care for His children any number of ways. In my life, I see that this is one way in which God provided.

Scripture tells us that God's timing and His ways are always best. "For my thoughts are not your thoughts, neither are your ways my ways, declares the Lord. As the heavens are higher than the earth, so are my ways higher than your ways and my thoughts than your thoughts." (Isa. 55:8, 9 NIV) We each have a choice as to what we believe. It is very easy to get into a "poor me pity mode" and say:

"Why is this happening to me now?"

"Could You not have done this another way, God?"

"I do not like this at all and I am really mad at You!"

"Obviously, you do not care about me, God."

"You must not be a very big God if you could not stop this from happening."

Some of these are actual statements I have said myself. Others, people have mentioned to me through their own grief journeys. I also believe that He is big enough to handle our questions, hurt, and angry words. He knows our heartache so there is really little point in hiding it and pretending it is not there.

Go ahead and tell God how you feel. Lay it out there for Him to hear and get it off your chest. You will notice a load lifted from your shoulders as well as a renewing and freeing of your heart. After sharing with God how you really feel, be ready to take the next step forward. Do not allow your grief and anger to fester and spoil the future He has for you. As you release your feelings and pour them out to God, He wants to take them and bring you healing, relief, and eventually joy.

There is no prescribed time of healing that is right for everyone. Each person's journey through grief will be unique. Try not to judge each other as you grieve with family and friends over the loss of a loved one. The important thing for you to examine and watch for is that you move forward, however quickly or slowly that may be. It saddens me to know of some people who fail to get over their loss and instead stubbornly hold onto their anger with God for years. Dropping out of church, refusing to pray, or failing to read the Bible will only cause you to feel more lost and alone.

Do not get discouraged when you think you are doing fine and then all of a sudden you have a sad day. Those days will come along. Do not feel as if you are not making progress or fear that your sadness will last forever. I know I will always miss Alan and I still feel sad plenty of days. I cannot truly say that I am happy yet. However, I am working through my loss and I trust that God is in control. In His timing, I am going to feel better more often and grow stronger each day by leaning on Him and learning to be content with my life. As the apostle, Paul, wrote in the Bible, "I know what it is to be in need, and I know what it is to have plenty. I have learned the secret of being content in any and every situation, whether well fed or hungry, whether living in plenty or in want." (Phil. 4:12 NIV)

God's timing is perfect, Dear One. It is not easily understood by our finite, human minds, but you can trust this to be true as you wait upon His perfect timing in your life.

Your fellow journeyer,

Karen

Application:

> Compile a list of those situations that are out of your control. Perhaps it will be useful for you to write those items on paper and then physically place them in your Bible or at the foot of a cross, symbolizing that you are giving that list over to God. Remember, He can handle all things so it makes sense to release the chaos and difficulties to Him.

> Now list what you do have control over in your life. Do you spend a large amount of time watching television? Is the computer something you spend hours on daily? Do you make the choice to exercise and take care of yourself? Eating healthy, regular meals is necessary to stay well. Knowing that you do have control over parts of your life will help with the hopelessness you may feel at times.

> Pray and ask God for a special, trusted friend that can be there for you no matter what. Someone that you can call or text and say, "Hey, I am feeling sad today." Or find a person to whom you can admit, "I cannot stop crying today." This person does not need to try and fix your

situation. They need only be willing to listen and love you through those low moments you are bound to experience.

I recommend choosing a friend of your same gender to fill this role. We need to guard our hearts through this difficult journey and not open up too quickly to certain types of contact when we may be vulnerable. We are not always good judges of relationships when our grief is new and we may be prone to form attachments that are either unhealthy for us or for the other person.

CHAPTER 6

There is No Perfect Substitute – Or is There?

Dear One,

As I begin this chapter, I am anticipating and dreading the dental surgery that I will have in the morning. In the past, I have endured numerous procedures on various parts of my mouth. Tomorrow I am having a tooth pulled and bone grafting begun for a dental implant. I really dislike going to the dentist and having my mouth worked on. With that being said, I am missing Alan tonight.

A friend of mine is taking me to the appointment since I will be unable to drive with the "relaxing" medication I will be given for the procedure. While she is a wonderful friend, she is not my husband.

As I traveled home this evening from work, the Pastor-On-Call at the church contacted me and offered to come in the morning to pray with me. I told him it was not necessary and that I would be fine. I realize the busyness of his schedule. Even if he had come, he too is not my husband.

I stopped at the store tonight to make sure I would have a sufficient amount of juice, yogurt, and other soft foods in the refrigerator. The next couple of days I will be unable to get out and I must provide for myself. While I am very capable of running that shopping errand, it is not my husband doing it for me.

What I am trying to say is there really is no perfect substitute when it comes to the people we love and the people we miss. No one can take Alan's place. He was a very special part of my life. He had known me for more than three decades and could read my thoughts with great accuracy. We shared special moments and held memories that no one else will ever know. Like most married couples we had funny stories, secrets, and awkward mistakes which were too embarrassing to share with others. Perhaps you too are missing a person that held these qualities for you.

Even though there is no substitute for Alan in my life, that does not mean that I am doomed to live in sadness, with emptiness and unending tears. There is not another who will be a perfect substitute for my husband. No one can put life back the way it was before his death. Yet, there is Someone who knows all about substitution!

This Someone is Jesus Christ. He has been waiting for us to realize our need for Him since the beginning of time. Jesus is the expert at being a substitute. In fact, He alone can fit the description of "the perfect substitute."

We are all doomed to eternal life in Hell because we are born sinners. Genesis 3 explains how life on earth changed from beautiful and perfect to disfigured and destroyed. The act of disobedience when Adam and Eve ate the forbidden fruit caused sin to enter into the world. With that sin came hurt, hatred, hardship, and hopelessness as mankind was now destined to a life separated from God.

Thankfully, God loved His creation too much to leave us alone in this broken world. He already had a plan to reconcile our relationship with Him and to provide forgiveness. His plan is explained by the apostle John who wrote, "For God so loved the world that he gave his one and only Son, that whoever believes in him shall not perish but have eternal life." (John 3:16 NIV) In order for you and me to receive that forgiveness required to spend eternity in Heaven, we must first acknowledge and accept the sacrifice that Christ made for each of us. By realizing that only Jesus Christ can meet our needs, we come to understand that He has to be our "perfect substitute." As He forgives, we in turn receive eternal life with God.

While I miss Alan, especially when I am facing the unpleasant things of life, I know that he has already been given the gift of Heaven. As a child, Alan accepted Jesus as His personal Lord and Savior, making Him Alan's "perfect substitute."

I will continue to miss Alan and be reminded that he cannot be replaced when it comes to certain earthly needs. At the same time, I can praise God that I know the "perfect substitute" for all of my spiritual needs. While I look forward to the day I will be in Heaven, today I am grateful for friends who help me the best they know how.

Your fellow journeyer,

Karen

Application:

> ➤ Who are the people in your life that help you? You might find it useful to begin a list so you know whom you can contact when assistance is needed.
>
> ➤ Now, in the spirit of giving back and focusing on others, try to write a note to each person on your list, thanking them for helping you.
>
> ➤ Take an inventory of what you are allowing in your life as a substitution for the time you spent with your loved one. Is it a healthy activity or hobby? Is it time well spent? If not, pray and ask God how you might make better choices with your time and your energy.
>
> ➤ Have you accepted the substitution that Jesus Christ has willingly provided for you by dying on the cross? If you have further questions on this topic, turn to the last chapter of this book, "Meeting Jesus" to see God's plan for salvation.

CHAPTER 7

Is This Dream
My Reality?

Dear One,

This journey of grief is certainly dreamlike at times. Not the kind of dream you yearn for or look forward to; but the kind of dream that does not seem possible or real. Often I wake up in bed and turn toward Alan's empty side, having my breath taken away as I realize that he really is not there.

I have thought far too many times, "Wait until I tell Alan" only to remember I am not able to. How wonderful it would be to converse and hear his comments on things like the new overpass on the highway, my new hairstyle, or the big storm that just hit the east coast. Just as in any partnership, you long to see things through each other's eyes.

There are life events I feel he is missing. He is not here for our youngest son's senior recital in college, the marriage of our oldest son, or the death of our dear friend. It is bittersweet to image what Alan would say to decisions I have made these past few years: the renovation of our master bathroom, shopping for a new car, updating the lawn, and pulling out that ugly bush we hated. While I believe he would actually be proud of me, it makes me sad that circumstances have made it necessary to function on my own.

My head assures me that Alan really is not sad about missing things here. How could you long for the things of earth, which pale in comparison to the glory and wonder of Heaven? The apostle, Paul, tells us that Heaven is better and he "would prefer to be away from the body and at home with the Lord." (2 Cor. 5:8 NIV) Intellectually I know that Alan is not missing anything. He is living the ultimate dream of a lifetime in Heaven. I can be sure of this because of the personal relationship he had with Jesus Christ.

While I have head knowledge that tells me where Alan now resides, it is my heart that sometimes confuses me. Convincing my heart of what my head knows is the challenge. While I may feel I am living a dream, it is actually my reality. My husband is no longer here with me. He is not by my side while I make difficult decisions.

It is often hard for me to enjoy doing the fun things in life instead of feeling guilty. The enemy, Satan, wants to keep us locked away in lonely isolation. I know I have a right to smile. Alan would want me to laugh and live my life well, treasuring each opportunity that presents itself. I am not always sure how to go about doing that, but I am learning to trust that God is going to bless me as I grow and move forward in my grief journey.

In finishing up Beth Moore's Bible Study entitled *The Patriarchs*,[3] she states, "Beloved, in God's economy fruitfulness trumps forgetfulness every time. No matter how differently we feel at times, becoming fruitful in our troubles has far greater ramifications of blessing than forgetting our troubles." Allowing

God to use me and bless others through my journey is part of being fruitful. My choice is to remember, endure, and live through the pain of missing my loved one in order to live out my new reality. No, my life is not a dream now, but I do dream of a time in the future when I too will be with Christ in Heaven. Alan will also be there waiting for me. I can even imagine him cheering me on some days, saying, "I am so proud of you! I knew you could do this without me!"

Your fellow journeyer,

Karen

Application:

> ➢ Does your life seem unreal and dreamlike at times? In the midst of navigating your new reality, is it possible to find some joy in remembering good times with your loved one? Making a picture album of some favorite times together can be a great way to recall pleasant memories.
> ➢ Realize that the moments you temporarily forget your loved one is gone can serve as reminders of the unique relationship you had. Rejoice in that! Not everyone has the opportunity to enjoy special times with loved ones – past or present. Make the most of your current relationships. Enjoy building new memories together.
> ➢ Begin a journal if you have not already. Record the moments you wish you could share. Write out those conversations you would have with your loved one. As you continue on your journey, you may find comfort in looking back and seeing God's provision and blessings.

CHAPTER 8

Triggers, Those Little Reminders

Dear One,

I just could not figure out what was wrong with me. Once again, I found myself crying all the time. The progress I had made in my grief journey appeared to have come to a halt. I was frustrated and embarrassed that I seemed to be falling apart again. Did this mean my faith was not strong enough? Was I not trusting God with my walk through this incredibly difficult time of life? What had changed? What was different this week from last week to make me feel like this? Then the answer came to me. I was preparing to leave on a trip for work and realized I was stressing out over the details.

Traveling is a trigger for me. A trigger is an event or item that brings about a memory. It has taken a while to discover that when I have a trip coming up, whether it is for business or pleasure, I find myself dealing with more tears and emotions as the departure date approaches.

Traveling can place me in a vulnerable position because I will be working with people I do not know from around the country. What if they ask me questions about my family? How am I expected to answer without falling apart? The sadness and pain will rise to the surface again, placing everyone in an uncomfortable position.

To avoid the awkwardness in these situations, I find myself withdrawing. No longer am I a carefree and fun-loving person, able to laugh and joke with new friends. Instead, I find I am more reserved, unwilling to risk hurt or judgment from others. My tendency to volunteer and take the lead occurs less often and I am not as eager to try new things. In time, I know I will regain my confidence and be able to step up and be "more myself." For now though, I find it difficult to deal with the surprises that can arise in new situations.

How do I handle my triggers? One way is by coveting the prayers of others. I recently shared with several friends what I had discovered about my traveling trigger. It touched my heart that one of them later pulled me aside and said that she was praying for me and asked how I was dealing with my upcoming trip. Her expressed concern made me feel extremely blessed. Having people pray for us is vital. In fact Scripture says to intercede for one another. "And pray in the Spirit on all occasions with all kinds of prayers and requests. With this in mind, be alert and always keep on praying for all the saints." (Eph. 6:18 NIV)

Another helpful tip in dealing with triggers is to keep busy and not allow yourself time to overthink an upcoming trip. I am not suggesting that you avoid or hide your feelings. What I am proposing is that it may not be wise to have too much free time to fret and worry prior to a trip. Satan, our enemy, is less able to occupy our thoughts with pain, sadness, and fear when we are focusing on people, tasks, and ministry.

Being aware of our triggers is another way of managing. Recognizing them is helpful in combatting and preparing so as not to be blindsided when the associated feelings arise. Even though raw emotions may appear, take heart, for their power is lessened when they are not a surprise.

I wish I could say the only cause of stress for me is traveling. So far, I have come to recognize these other items as triggers too:

The thirtieth of each month – which is the day Alan passed away.

Special days of celebration such as birthdays and anniversaries are hard.

Talking to certain people who bring up specific memories.

Running across forgotten items in our home that hold special meaning.

We can expect that multiple triggers will be discovered as we work through grief. When we expose those, God will provide us with the ability to push through the surprise, sadness, and tears they can create while we continue to move forward toward healing.

Your fellow journeyer,

Karen

Application:

> Have you found yourself crying more at certain times? Keep a journal to list the flow of your emotions so you can discover certain patterns. Find a friend or two with whom you may confide in comfortably. These may be people who walk a similar journey to your own and can

be very helpful in providing insight. The Holy Spirit can provide that in a person. I have a few great friends from my local Grief Share group that are a solid "sounding board" and support for me.

➢ You may find it useful to make a chart marking your progress through grief. Each week notate how you feel. Perhaps you see yourself moving from sad to glad and then back to sad again. Remember it takes time to see steady improvement.

Grief cannot be avoided. I encourage you to move through your difficulty and loss today in order to walk a healthy grief journey. Otherwise, you may find yourself dealing with your loss years from now, realizing you have wasted precious time. Do not be afraid to acknowledge and work through your sadness and pain. Move at your own pace. After all, it is your journey.

➢ When you begin to recognize your triggers, use that knowledge to help you cope and move forward as you embrace them rather than fear them. Know that God desires to give you strength.

➢ I encourage you not to worry or be anxious concerning questions people may ask about your loved one. I have found that the actual conversation is usually not as bad as what I have imagined. It helps to be prepared and have in mind some simple answers that you can say in response to their questions. Be assured, Dear One, you really are not required to explain any more than you desire. It is okay to just quietly say you would rather not discuss it at that time.

CHAPTER 9

Flying Among the Clouds – Am I Closer to You Up Here?

Dear One,

On a recent flight, I found myself looking out the window as we flew above the clouds, intently looking for a sign that I was somehow closer to Heaven. This may sound a bit silly to you, but it was not the first time the thought had occurred to me. Perhaps you too have experienced trying to "see" your loved one in the wonder of the clouds.

A couple of years ago I read a few books on Heaven. While I found some of the information to be useful, there is much of that material that I take cautiously. The Word of God, the Bible, is truly the only firm and faultless source we have teaching us about Heaven. What can we learn from the Bible about this place and our loved ones being there? Here are a few things you can know.

The Bible reveals that if our loved ones truly had a personal relationship with Jesus Christ, then they are indeed in Heaven awaiting our arrival. The relationship I write of indicates that at some point in their life, they understood their own human condition of sinfulness and being separated from a holy and perfect God. Upon this realization, they also recognized that only Jesus Christ could provide forgiveness while restoring a relationship with God. Acting upon this realization, they then accepted Jesus as their own personal Lord and Savior.

We also read in the Bible that people do not get to go to Heaven simply by being good and doing good things. The standard set by God to enter Heaven is perfection. None of us can achieve that level of faultlessness on our own. We must rely upon the perfect sacrifice of Jesus Christ who loved us enough to bridge that gap – from sin to perfection.

To be absent from the body is to be with God in Heaven. Paul wrote, "We are confident, I say, and would prefer to be away from the body and at home with the Lord." (2 Cor. 5:8 NIV) When I tearfully said good-bye to Alan at the graveside, I knew in my head that he really was not in that beautiful casket, but had already begun to enjoy an incredible life in Heaven in the very presence of God. While my heart hurt and I sobbed as I forced myself to leave, I have the assurance that I did not leave him in a cold and forsaken state.

Scripture leads us to understand that Heaven is upward. It describes the ascension, or taking up, of Jesus. "After He said this, He was taken up before their very eyes, and a cloud hid Him from their sight." (Acts 1:9 NIV) There are other references implying that the direction of Heaven is up. "Who knows if the human spirit rises upward and if the spirit of the animal goes down into the earth?" (Eccl. 3:21 NIV) In another it reads, "I press on toward the goal to win the prize for which God has called me heavenward in Christ Jesus." (Phil 3:14 NIV) Scriptures like these propel me to wonder about being closer to Heaven when flying above the clouds. I smile at the possibility.

I know that Heaven exists and I am grateful that I do not have to be above the clouds to feel close to God. I am able to stay near Him in my everyday life: in church, in Bible Study, in the quiet reading of His Word, and in constantly talking to Him in prayer.

There have been times I have spoken out loud to Alan, although I doubt he hears me. Speaking to Alan is more therapeutic for me and plays a part in my grief journey since I had been able to talk to him daily for over 30 years. It is important to understand that I do not pray to my husband. I pray only to God, for God alone is the One who deserves our worship and He alone can answer our prayers.

While I may not see God with my eyes each day, I do see evidence of His daily presence in my life. It is up to me to be confident that God is near and to be comforted by that knowledge. "I am my Beloved's and He is mine." (Song of Solomon 6:3 King James Version)

Your fellow journeyer,

Karen

Application:

> Are there certain times when you feel closer to your loved one? When you feel these special times, relish the good memories they create. Perhaps gather certain pictures or mementos and place them in a special box that can be easily accessed when you need to feel near them.

Scripture cautions us against participating in séances. If you are tempted to actually try to contact your loved one in this way, please stop and do not fall victim to those who displease God with this type of sorcery. "When you enter the land the Lord your God is giving you, do not learn to imitate the detestable ways of the nations there. Let no one be found among you who sacrifices their son or daughter in the fire, who practices divination or sorcery, interprets omens, engages in witchcraft, or casts spells, or who is a medium or spiritist or who consults the dead. (Deut. 18:9–11 NIV)

➤ Spend some time processing and thinking back on your favorite moments with your loved one. Write those in your journal so that you can go back and recall those memories. I have found that remembering special times together gives me a sense of comfort and closeness.

➤ Take inventory on where you stand spiritually. Do you have that personal relationship with Jesus Christ yourself, and feel assured of being ushered into His Presence upon your own passing?

➤ If you are inclined to do some reading on the topic of Heaven, be careful as to your selection of books. The information placed in them must agree with and never contradict the Bible. Randy Alcorn's book, *Heaven*[4] is a good source with which to begin. However, my recommendation is to stick with the Bible being your main reading on this subject.

CHAPTER 10

Where Is The Joy?

Dear One,

All my life I have been taught that as a child of God, I will have joy. I used to equate joy with happiness, good times, and having fun. I no longer define it quite that way. Instead, I believe joy is a much deeper emotion. When possessed clearly and correctly, joy is not easily shaken.

The emotion that is most often confused with joy is happiness. I do not believe they are synonyms though since happiness tends to be dependent upon our situation. When we are in a good place in life, we feel great and are certainly happy about it. "Let the good times roll" is an expression from years ago. I suppose that is all well and good, but what happens when the good times have come to a sudden stop and they no longer "roll?" What happens when they gradually fade into the past and the present is much darker and more difficult that you ever imagined? Then happiness tends to give way to discontentment, sadness, and dissatisfaction.

Joy can be different. However, if we are placing our joy in temporary things, then we can be sure that it will be just as fleeting as the happiness described. If my joy is placed in my family or my job or my hobby, then I am in serious danger of lacking the true lasting joy that Scripture describes. "Do not grieve, for the joy of the Lord is your strength." (Neh. 8:10 NIV) True joy comes from God.

This Scripture speaks of the joy that comes not from what I do, but from what has been done for me and who I am now. God has taken me to be His child. Because of God's great love and provision for each of us, we can possess a joy that the world, with all its faults, cannot whisk away, either suddenly or over a period of time.

The enemy would want us to believe that our joy comes from being a success, having money, fame, and plenty of material possessions. But Scripture warns us of that type of lifestyle. "Do not store up for yourselves treasures on earth, where moth and rust destroy and where thieves break in and steal. But store up for yourselves treasures in Heaven...For where your treasure is, there your heart will be also." (Matt. 6:19–21 NIV)

The exciting thing about the joy that comes from knowing Jesus is that we do not have to wait to arrive in Heaven to possess and experience that joy. We can have it right here, right now. Being sad is not the same thing as living without joy. I have been sad plenty of days and I know I will still be sad in the future as life continues to throw difficulties my way. However, in the midst of all the trials and pain, I do not have to be without my joy because it is rooted in my faith in God.

This leads to another contrast between happiness and joy – its origin. I do not believe joy is just what we feel. Joy is also what I know deep within my soul. It is like the child's song about having joy in my heart. Even in the midst of my darkest days, I would adamantly testify that I still possessed it. That joy of my salvation is something that I refuse to relinquish or deny. I can have it and shed my tears at the same time.

Do I hope to smile more someday? Of course! Do I desire to be spontaneous again and have fun in the future? Absolutely. Let me share with you a portion of what I wrote in my journal only one short year after Alan died. As you read it, study it for the presence of joy and hope.

> "I believe I can still function and I get up in the morning only because I manage to keep my focus on Jesus. Sure, there are times I take my eyes off Him and get scared thinking about my list of stresses and the changes I have suffered. But then I remember what I've been taught and what I've known for so long. That God is faithful; God is good all the time; God is all I need. When I don't know exactly what to do, I do the only thing I know to do – trust Him and keep putting one foot in front of the other. I'm not sure when I'll be happy again. But, I do know my joy comes from my relationship with Christ. And I'm learning that Jesus has to be sufficient for me. That's not settling for less– that's my reality and that's the best for me."

So Dear One, when you struggle with your emotions and feel you cannot possibly survive the way life is now, remember you can get through this difficult time. Allow God to comfort and guide you. Trust Him, perhaps more than you have ever trusted anyone before. He will see you through this difficult journey. Maybe the path will not be the way that you have pictured or imagined. Things are seldom as we envision them. Know that the direction in which God is leading is even better and serves a greater purpose than the course you can visualize.

I would like to close this chapter with a portion of Scripture that has touched my heart dearly over the last few years. "Because of the Lord's great love we are not consumed, for his compassions never fail. They are new every morning; great is your faithfulness. I say to myself, The Lord is my portion; therefore I will wait for him." (Lam. 3:22–24 NIV)

No matter how hard our day has been, God's great love for us will keep us from being consumed by our sadness, despair, and grief. Every morning we can count on having more than enough from God to sustain us. He will enable us to move forward on our grief journeys. We have the assurance that joy will be available to us. We may not see it immediately, but take heart, Dear One. It is there. "...his favor lasts a lifetime; weeping may remain for a night, but rejoicing comes in the morning." (Ps. 30:5 NIV)

Your fellow journeyer,
Karen

Application:

> List the things that make you happy. After completing this, go through your list again and examine it a second time, placing a check by the things that are temporary and will not last. Realize that those checked items will go away or change at some point, possibly causing you sadness and heartache.

➢ Now make a list of the things that bring you joy. Remember, these should not be dependent upon circumstances or life conditions. I will give you two of mine to get you started, as I realize it may be difficult to think clearly and see blessings right now, deep in the midst of your own grief.

    o   I have joy in my salvation through Jesus Christ
    o   I find great joy in my ministry to children and parents

You may find it useful to read through some Scriptures outlining joy. I have listed some of my favorites in the back of this book to get you started.

CHAPTER 11

Does This Get Easier?

Dear One,

When we are in the midst of doing something difficult, we tend to focus on completing the task and being able to put it behind us. There is a great sense of relief and satisfaction when we arrive on the other side of hard times. How does that work when we are maneuvering our way through grief? Does this journey ever end? Can we see a light at the end of the tunnel? Are we promised laughter and happier times?

Well, Dear One, no one is promised an easy life here on this earth. From the time sin entered the world in the Garden of Eden, not only do people now get sick and die, but the earth itself is deteriorating. Nothing will ever be perfect again here on this planet. Even with our relationship in Christ and the assurance that He is our salvation, the very foundation on which we stand, we are not promised that life will be easy and full of continual happiness and good times. This statement, however, is not news to you. The grief you are experiencing is evidence of this fact. You may even be asking, "Is this ever going to end?" I want to encourage you with a resounding, "Yes!"

Your grief will not last forever. During the first days, months, and even years, you may feel as if you will never smile or laugh from deep within your soul again. There will be times when you surprisingly find yourself managing a smile or giggling about something. You may feel guilty, as if you are wrong to enjoy a lightening of your mood and sorrow, if only for a moment.

The Bible addresses the issue of guilt. We read in Romans 8:1 that there is no condemnation in Christ. God is not there to crack a whip over us if we say or do something wrong. I believe the Holy Spirit is given to us, as children of God, to help guide and correct our actions as needed. He provides the quickening of our spirit in order to encourage and teach us as we live to honor Him. The guilt we feel accusing us is not from God. There is nothing wrong with having fun and enjoying our life again. The enemy is working hard to defeat you and steal the joy that is rightfully yours in Christ by pushing guilt upon you. You do not have to accept that.

I know there have been times early in my grief when I scolded myself for enjoying a show, or having dinner out with friends. Being in the company of others was something I had to relearn and give myself permission to enjoy. You too may need to be reminded that guilt is not from God.

I think it is important, however, to realize that while guilt is not from God, conviction is. This is the feeling you get when you know you are doing something that goes against God and His commands. As a Christian, the Holy Spirit is "convicting you" and speaking to your heart. It is His job to guide you in making better choices with your life and attitude.

If, however, you are living the best you know how, yet still feel badly, pray and ask God whether this is guilt or conviction.

Seeking wise counsel from godly friends may help you discern between the two as well.

At this moment I am sitting in a hotel room writing this chapter, enjoying a break from a conference where I am volunteering. I saw a friend yesterday that I only see once or twice a year. We manage to follow and keep up with each other on social networks. In greeting me, he smiled with tears in his eyes and commented that he was so proud of me for doing well in my grief journey. He could see the improvement and joy in my life again.

Had we not been surrounded by hundreds of people at that moment, I may have started crying. His comment meant so much to me. It showed that I am making progress in my grief. I am closer to the end of the journey than I was three years ago. I have the opportunity to give glory to God for allowing me the strength, tenacity, and fortitude to continue forward with my life.

Dear One, the world does not stop for us, though we wish it would. We may resent that after only a few weeks, others seemingly forget about us. They move back to enjoying their lives while we are stuck with our grief and struggle to place one foot in front of the other on a daily basis. My friend's comment encouraged me. I am not stuck but am making progress and others can see it!

I believe God uses our friends and family in special ways to send little messages of love and support. Picture your loved ones standing on either side of a running path with their arms raised in the air, clapping, and cheering for you. Hear their encouragement that you can indeed do this! With the help of a loving, capable, all-knowing God, you will survive this loss and see that you too, can make progress and move forward.

Your fellow journeyer,

Karen

Application:

> Look back over your life before your grief journey and write down some of the challenges you encountered and how you made it through those. You may have to go back to your childhood to get started. After you have completed this, praise God for allowing you to get through those hard times. Realize that He is the same God today, capable of helping you in your grief.

> Research some verses on being "victorious in Christ," allowing them to remind you that we are not created to live life alone. God wants to provide us with the help we need. A verse you can begin with is 1 John 5:4. It tells us to rejoice because we can overcome the world with Christ! Now, you begin your own list. Let God speak to you as you read, study, and learn.

> Write down your goals. What are they? They may be as simple as getting up in the morning or remembering to eat three times a day. Perhaps you would like to venture out on your own, even for a small errand. I want to encourage you to aim high. Ask God to help you not only enjoy the goals you set, but the journey toward them, realizing that each day is a gift from God. Painful as they may be, He has a purpose for you in each and every one of them.

CHAPTER 12

Why So Shy?

Dear One,

I have never been a very out-going person. Introvert better describes me - a person who likes to process life while sitting back to watch people. As an adult though, I have learned to "work the crowd" at a gathering and be comfortable talking to new acquaintances.

Isolation is a real temptation in early grief. I realize that it would be easy for me to just remain in the house by myself and not interact with people for long periods of time. This is not always a negative trait. Being alone can allow for productive work to occur. However, it can be detrimental to take a solitary lifestyle too far and become hermit-like. Knowing why we prefer to be by ourselves is a start to understanding what we truly need and why we require it.

Being alone tends to be an easy out for me now. At times I dread leaving the house. Having the convenience of a constant companion for nearly thirty years has spoiled me. I had a friend suggest that perhaps through the years of marriage I had begun to think of myself almost as an extension of Alan, rather than an individual person. I think that may be an accurate analysis.

We were a pair, a couple, and now suddenly part of me is gone. Isolation may be attractive but it is not always healthy.

Another instance of isolating behavior can be seen in self-inflicted social exclusion. Partaking in small talk with a group of people is difficult. I prefer to listen to others chat rather than contributing to the banter. I figure it is safer to "hide away" in a crowd. Continuing to separate from others will not help us move forward, though. We must learn to once again give away part of ourselves with others through conversations.

I think it is helpful to know what we are willing to share with others and what we prefer to keep private. The choice is yours as to how open and vulnerable you are with people. No one can or should expect any more of you. This is your journey and you get to set the boundaries.

I have found it helpful to have answers to common questions prepared ahead of time. It takes away part of the fear and anxiety I may feel in social situations. When we have those boundaries in place, we are not expending unnecessary energy guessing and dreading what the next topic or question may be.

There will be some people who are easier to talk to than others. I recall that four weeks after Alan's death, I was at church watching rehearsal for a Christmas program. Our new music pastor's wife came and sat down quietly to express her condolences. She never got to meet Alan. Yet, her gentle attitude instantly put me at ease. I sensed she neither wanted nor expected anything from me. She has since been an easy person for me to approach.

There are other people to whom I am not yet ready to reveal everything. They are more like acquaintances that I keep at an arm's length. While this may sound rude, I do it in order to feel safe and in control. There will always be people in this world who thrive on drama and the misfortune of others. These are the people I now tend to avoid.

The distance I create is a defense mechanism to avoid pain and possible embarrassment. While we can do our best to dodge pain, it will occasionally appear when we do not expect it and oftentimes, when it is least convenient. I have come to realize that avoiding people and conversations has not always been helpful in moving through grief. It has created a vacuum in which I live and a loneliness that intensifies the sadness. Hopefully my mistakes will help you avoid harmful habits in your own life.

Now that I have learned what the problem is, how do I fix it? I cannot, but that does not mean it is a hopeless situation. While I may not be able to fix it, God can. Paul wrote, "I can do everything through Him who gives me strength." (Phil. 4:13 NIV) I can do anything with God's help, which includes surviving and learning to grow in new situations and in meeting new people. That verse is actually written just after Paul stated that he had learned to be content in all circumstances. "I have learned the secret of being content in any and every situation, whether well fed or hungry, whether living in plenty or in want." (Phil. 4:12 NIV)

Learning to be content now as a widow is the secret to being able to do hard things. As I learn to accept the journey God has given me today, I can get over the fear of sharing about myself to others in the future.

I am not saying that all the pain is gone. It still hurts me to answer, "He passed away twenty-six months ago." While his passing is still surreal for me at times, I am able to make that statement out loud and not care quite so much what the other person is thinking. I do not speak to gain pity nor do I want to talk about my grief in depth with strangers. When I do share, it is with people I trust, whether they are old friends or new acquaintances.

I have a wise supervisor who supports me and has taught me an important tip. We had a temporary preacher coming to speak for a while at the church where I am on staff. I dreaded the lunch we were to have with this man to get to know him. Thinking of questions I might have to answer unnerved me. Then I learned that my supervisor had already informed the preacher a little about my journey and situation. He reasoned he never wanted to cause me pain or place the other person in a compromising situation of discomfort and regret. I loved that!

I am not saying that others should go around and tell everyone the details about your loss. My suggestion though, is to give permission to a trusted friend to pave the way by sharing a little about your journey with others if the need arises. Knowing that you will not be placed in an awkward situation will provide you relief from stress as you socialize more. The day will come when you will feel like sharing on your own. Until then, may God give you a peace and comfort with special friends to lighten your load and anxiety. Learn to walk boldly, relying upon Him.

Your fellow journeyer,

Karen

Application:

> Determine what it is that you want others to know. Write those things down and share them with someone you can

trust. Allow them permission to give that information to new people when necessary.

➢ Ask God for special friends to play the role of your protector and advocate when needed. There may be times you need others to create a diversion in order to keep your boundaries intact. Be sure they are clear on what it is that you want shared and what should remain private.

➢ Do some role-playing with a trusted friend. Have them begin a conversation as if meeting you for the first time. This practice can help you feel comfortable fielding questions that may arise from others.

➢ Honestly answer the question: "Am I isolating myself to the extent that it is unhealthy?" Have you been outside your home or work place just for fun lately? Plan a little "field trip" around town. If this is too hard to do alone, once again enlist a close friend to share in your adventure.

➢ Have you engaged in conversations with the people you encounter daily? Be intentional in doing so if you find yourself trying to "hide away" in a crowd. The more you practice this, the easier it will become.

CHAPTER 13

Regrets and The Danger of "What If"

Dear One,

"Cast all your anxiety on Him because He cares for you." (1 Pet. 5:7 NIV) Holding onto our worries is an unnecessary task. "Do not be anxious about anything, but in everything by prayer and petition with thanksgiving, present your requests to God." (Phil. 4:6 NIV) Scripture tells us not to worry. We have the ability to place our cares and needs before a very real, living God. Why then do we spend our time and energy on things we cannot change?

As I think back over the many years of marriage I had with Alan, I can easily pick out times when I could have done better. My words should have been kinder, my attitude not as frustrated, and my life less rushed. We had a good marriage, but it certainly was not perfect. Perfection this side of Heaven is a myth. That does not mean we do not strive to do our best to improve and be a better person. Scripture calls this becoming more like Christ. John 3:30 explains, "He must become greater; I must become less." I once had a pastor who is remembered for saying it this way: "Not I, but Christ!"

While God's Word teaches us how to continually improve at putting Christ first and foremost in our lives and in the decisions we make, it is important to give ourselves grace. We all need a break and to realize that there will be times when we fail. Be careful, though, to not use the giving of grace as a reason to make excuses for yourself. Apologize when you should, admit your shortcomings, and prayerfully work on them.

Dear One, do not spend your time in this grief journey beating yourself up with the question, "What if?" We have no power to go back and change anything. I could easily ask myself:

"What if I had been home sooner?"

"What if I had kept talking to him on the phone that day so I could dial 911 immediately?"

"What if we had made better choices regarding food over the years?"

"What if I had insisted more on good exercise routines together?"

The list could go on and on.

There may be people around you who try to ask the "What ifs" for you. I have a family member, who in her grief, had screamed at me on the phone the day after Alan's death, "If only you had…" I immediately cut her off and quickly ended the conversation. The last thing I needed at that point was to accept blame when it was not mine to own. Dear One, if you feel responsible somehow for the reason you are on this journey of grief, I encourage you to seek wise counsel. They can show you how to clearly evaluate a situation and how to forgive others as well as yourself if needed.

I love the lesson to be learned in the story of how Jesus walked on the water in the midst of a storm. His disciples were in a boat, late at night. They saw Jesus walking on the water and became terrified, thinking He was a ghost. Jesus spoke and reassured them, calming their fears. Then the impulsive disciple, Peter, spoke up. "'Lord, if it's you,' Peter replied, 'tell me to come to you on the water.' 'Come,' He said. Then Peter got down out of the boat, walked on the water and came toward Jesus. But when he saw the wind, he was afraid and, beginning to sink, cried out, 'Lord, save me!'" (Matt. 14:28–31 NIV)

Just as Peter successfully walked on the water while his eyes were on the Savior, we too can maneuver successfully through our journey only when we choose to look at Christ. When we take our eyes off Jesus and look instead at the things that scare us, we lose our concentration. Our attention is placed on the wrong things in life and we falter. Let Him be your focus. Receive from Him your strength and motivation to get up each day and move forward.

Do not believe the lies of the enemy who wants to see you defeated. Your life contains blessings, so be thankful. There is hope in your journey. It may be buried down deep and impossible to see at times. I promise you, it is there. How can I make that promise without even knowing you? It is because I know the Savior. I know and believe God's Word that tells us about the hope and the future we have as children of God.

One of my favorite Scriptures reads, "For I know the plans I have for you, declares the Lord, plans to prosper you and not to harm you, plans to give you hope and a future." (Jer. 29:11 NIV) God has not forgotten nor forsaken you, Dear One. He has a plan for you. Remember you are, and always will be, precious to Him.

No matter how you feel or what you do, God loves you and wants to care for you. There are times our choices do not allow His care and involvement in our lives. He is there waiting for you to realize that you are living life alone instead of leaning upon His good, strong hand.

There is an old hymn that I remember singing as a college student with friends. I still break out humming this song at times today, believing these words to be true and relevant. Helen Lemmel wrote the lyrics, "Turn your eyes upon Jesus, Look full in His wonderful face, And the things of earth will grow strangely dim, In the light of His glory and grace."[5]

Allow Christ to comfort you and remind you of the good times with your loved one when you begin to feel the attacks of the "What ifs." Give thought and energy to your future instead of wallowing in your past. None of us can change what has already happened. Instead, let us allow God to do His work today.

Your fellow journeyer,
Karen

Application:

> ➤ Recall and write down some special times that you had with your loved one. Perhaps it was time spent walking and talking in a park. Or maybe you were able to take a special trip together. As you record those wonderful memories, look to see if you have pictures of any of those places. Put together a collage of photos, ticket stubs, or concert programs you may have collected over the years. Placing these special items together in a frame can be a

fun and attractive way to display special memories to combat any "What ifs" you may later face.

➢ Spend time praising God for His provision and for His promise to never leave you. Give thanks that you have no cause for hopelessness with Him in your life.

➢ Choose to say "NO!" to regrets and "What Ifs" over which you are powerless, and "YES!" to the days ahead. With God's strength and power you can change and shape your future in a positive way.

CHAPTER 14

Uncharted Waters

Dear One,

Have you ever planned a trip somewhere, anticipated the travel, packed your car snacks and luggage, and buckled up for the ride only to realize you really were not sure of the exact roads to take? I did that recently. I plugged the destination into my trusty GPS, started the engine, backed out of the garage, and we were on our way. Or so I thought.

My son and I were headed down to visit the family gravesite where my husband is now buried along with his parents and grandparents. The cemetery is in another state and off the beaten path. I had not traveled to this family cemetery without my husband. He had always been the driver and navigator as I sat back to enjoy the ride, not really paying attention to the path we took to get there. Who knew I would have to remember these things?

The GPS took us to our destination, via a path that was anything but direct. This bazaar, unfamiliar route had me wondering for a while if we were really lost and if we had taken a wrong turn somewhere. Looking back on that crazy road trip and the misdirection we received, I began thinking about other unknowns and "uncharted waters" I have faced in the past few years.

The grief journey is certainly "uncharted waters" for those of us navigating it for the first time. I suspect, even if we have traveled this type of hurt before, the ride varies from loss to loss. So how do we get to our destination? Perhaps the more important question is what is our destination? Before we can arrive somewhere, we need to know where it is we are going. Easier said than done!

I can honestly say that I do not always feel certain about where I am headed. The destination Alan and I had planned as a couple was no longer an option. We had discussed our empty-nest years and retirement plans which included trips, our goals, life dreams, and the wishes we had shared. None of those ideas seemed to work for me now. While I will eventually retire and may do some traveling, it is hard to imagine what to expect now from my future.

Life does not stop for those of us on a grief journey. Nor do I think it should. Grief just has a way of changing those plans, goals, and dreams we had laid out for ourselves. No longer does the future seem crystal clear and exciting. Instead it is unknown and waiting to be redrawn. Our days and years now are "uncharted waters."

When explorers of long ago were discovering the new world, they were going to places where no one had yet traveled. I remember watching the adventures of Star Trek and hearing their famous line "boldly go where no man has gone before!" Dear One, the path you and I walk in our grief may feel like one that is untraveled, completely unknown, and for which there is no map. While this is true in a sense, it is important to remember that others have negotiated the grief journey quite well. They have survived and even learned to thrive and enjoy life. While their journeys are not the same as yours, I hope you find it encouraging seeing that there is hope and a positive destination in the path you are taking.

Each person's grief journey is a new adventure or unique voyage. While you are indeed traveling "uncharted waters," you have the opportunity to plan the journey yourself. While that may be a little overwhelming at first, I pray that you will also find it freeing and let your creative side explore and discover ways to enjoy your new path.

How have I planned my journey through "uncharted waters?" Alan and I never went to Disneyland together. Now, nearing the three-year anniversary of his death, I am beginning to plan a trip there, complete with Disney hotel. A friend of mine from church is a Disney expert and enthusiast and she will be accompanying me. She is also comfortable with my grief. My sudden tears do not bother her. Friendship with space is what she offers – not pity or unwanted mushy sentiment.

Has God placed anyone in your life like that; someone with whom you can enjoy new things? Do not be discouraged if you cannot name that person yet. Perhaps it is too soon for you to envision such a companion. Maybe you have not thought about planning the next stage of your grief journey to maneuver through your "uncharted waters." If I can do it, Dear One, I am positive you can. Use your imagination, summon your courage, and move forward. May you find smooth sailing on your next "uncharted waters".

Your fellow journeyer,

Karen

Application:

- ➤ What is it that you may had planned or dreamed of doing with your loved one, but did not get to accomplish? Is it possible to still follow through with those plans by changing a thing or two?
- ➤ Begin your plan. Where will you go? How will you get there? What does the path look like as you embark on this next leg of your journey? Make a checklist as you strategize so you can notate the progress you make.
- ➤ Visit a travel agency or AAA shop to pick up brochures on some possible destinations. Browse some websites to get ideas of places you would enjoy visiting and begin your list.
- ➤ Pray that God might bring just the right friend to come alongside as you dream and plan.

CHAPTER 15

When the Storms of Life Blow

Dear One,

My youngest son, Chris, and I recently arrived home after a quick trip to the Texas/Oklahoma panhandle area. We had the opportunity to get away and visit family for a few days. After catching a final lunch with everyone, our plan was to travel north on Highway 83 up through Garden City, Kansas. We had seen the clouds building for miles and I even mentioned earlier that I did not like the look of the sky. Having grown up in the Midwest, my weather-watching skills are pretty sharp. Sure enough, we were about fifteen miles south of I–70 when all of the sudden, the rain and vicious wind hit!

There were no sprinkles. There was no warning besides the ominous looking sky. The storm simply attacked. Even on the highest setting, my windshield wipers failed to keep up with the torrents of rain blown directly at us. We could not see the front of the car, much less the road. I slowed down and tried to drive, using the white stripe on the side of the pavement to guide us. Eventually, that too went away as I was blinded by the storm. I had no recourse but to pull over. Two other cars had done the same thing and we lined up behind them, turning on our hazard lights. Watching my rearview mirror, I prayed a car would not run into us.

We sat there for a couple of minutes before moving forward again, thinking it was getting better. The wind worsened though, and once again we were forced to pull over. I asked Chris to pull up the radar on his phone. To our horror, we saw that we were sitting in the middle of an intense storm, but were unable to tell how fast it was moving. The wind was horrendous, but I could not gauge how quickly it would end from that alone. We did know that the storm was moving southeast, yet it was impossible to guess the amount of time it would take to move away from where we sat.

All of the sudden, we heard then felt a huge bang. Chris jumped in his seat, yelled, and looked at me, thinking a car had hit us. Before I could explain what it was, the sky let loose and we were pelted with hail stones that were hitting so hard, I feared they would break my car window, cutting us both to pieces. The noise was so deafening we could not even hear each other speak.

I was nearly crying at this point, though I knew there was no time for tears. Instead, it was a time to take action! Not being one to sit in a bad, dangerous position for long, I made a decision. I stubbornly yelled to Chris that we had to get out of the storm, and the only way out was north. We pulled back on the road and determinedly crept along, watching that white stripe as it went in and out of my view with the rain, wind, and hail. There were times I nearly slowed down to a stop, especially when cars came from the other direction. I was praying hard, begging, and believing Jesus to calm the storm as he did for the disciples when he spoke, "Quiet! Be still!" (Mark 4:39 NIV)

Suddenly my phone began sounding with an alert that we were in a flood warning. I had already been concerned about flooding, as we had crawled across several small bridges. Chris just kept watching the radar and stayed silent. I am sure he too was praying hard as he watched me do my best to cope and get us to safety. I know I had a grim, determined look on my face and my hands were clenched, gripping the wheel, trying to keep the car on the road in the severe wind. Thankfully, the storm eventually began to lessen and we saw a break in the clouds.

We finally made it to I–70 and headed west for home, out of the storm. I am so very grateful to God for His provision and protection. I believe He alone saved us and kept us on the road when I was beside myself with fear and literally blinded to the road ahead. Thinking back on that journey, I realize that there was indeed a lesson to be found in that horrible driving experience.

So many times we are tossed into a "storm" of life that we must push through. While we may be tempted to check out, pull over, and refuse to live the life that is now ahead of us, we really must make a choice. We can choose to move backward, live in the past, and not face our reality. Perhaps we simply choose to sit in our "storm" and decline opportunities to move as we are paralyzed by the fear and pain we experience. Neither of these choices will move us where we need to go. However, we can choose to move forward, through the pain and unknowns of the road, and do our best to get out of the "storm" with God's help.

I would love to go back and live in the past, before my husband died. Yet there is no logic to this choice. The person I lived with is no longer here on this earth. The past cannot be recreated. So why not choose to live in reality?

It has become evident that living my current life without doing the work to move out of grief is not productive. If I fail to deal with the pain, fear, and loss experienced on this journey, I will only continue to feel tossed around and beaten by this storm in life.

Moving forward through the "storm" of grief is the best choice. We cannot ignore the truth that we are grieving. The fact that there has been loss and our life is now different is a truth that cannot be ignored. However, we can be brave, cling to God, and put one foot in front of the other to walk through the very thing that is frightening us and causing us so much pain.

I am so sorry you are hurting and I understand your pain and the desire you may have to just wish it all away. Wishes do not accomplish the work that the grief journey requires, though. You must attempt to move forward. Just as I did in the car, there will be times when you come to a stop or you slow down so much you wonder if you will ever make progress. You will, Dear One. Trust and have faith that God can help you do just that.

One of my favorite Scriptures states, "Do not fear, for I am with you; do not be dismayed, for I am your God. I will strengthen you and help you; I will uphold you with my righteous right hand." (Isa. 41:10 NIV) May you too, find strength for the days ahead with a very real, very powerful, and very loving God.

Your fellow journeyer,

Karen

Application:

> ➤ What frightens you? Admitting your fear and saying it out loud or writing it down can empower you to take a step to move forward, away from the very thing troubling you and making you anxious.

> ➤ Form a plan of action. Just as I realized I had to go north to get out of the wind, rain, and hail, what is it that you must do to begin your journey out of your "storm"? Perhaps you need to search for help. Maybe you need to pack away some items of the past in order to move ahead. Pray and ask God to show you how to navigate the stormy road you face. Then trust Him and follow His directions.

CHAPTER 16

Like a Segway

Dear One,

I had the opportunity to go to San Diego in February this past year for work. While there, my cousin came down from a nearby town and met me in the city to play for a day. We were walking around, sightseeing, and were headed to buy tickets for a harbor tour when a dozen Segway riders passed by. I suddenly heard myself shouting, "A Segway! I want to ride!" Sue and I continued walking when all of a sudden, the Segway tour guide turned around and pulled up beside me, handing me the vehicle. At first I was thrilled that my statement had received such results. Then I thought, "I have no idea how to do this!"

The tour guide had me hop on, instructed me to lean into the vehicle, showed a couple of basic maneuvers, and allowed me to move forward on my own about two hundred yards. It was great fun! Looking back on the experience, I can equate this to my grief journey in a couple of ways.

First, it really does pay to speak your mind at times. People around you will have a better idea of how to help, comfort, and allow you to heal if you are honest and brave enough to speak up.

Saying what is on your mind and in your heart can show others how to better meet your needs.

As we ask for help and let our needs be known, it is good to remember to be kind. There are ways for those of us grieving, to express ourselves so as not to harm the listener nor alienate them from wanting to be around us in the future. I will admit, at first I was not always tactful in revealing my thoughts and needs. With practice, I have improved at being honest without overwhelming friends. You too, will get better at this as you suggest to others how to help you.

I have also learned that in any new adventure, such as my Segway experience, we need to be willing to listen to instruction and try new things. Dear One, I feel that you are making headway just from your willingness to read this book and by allowing God to speak to you through my journey.

While I long to trust God and follow His instructions daily in all things, there are plenty of times when I seem to fail. I find it helpful to remember what God's Word teaches us. "Trust in the Lord with all your heart and lean not on your own understanding; in all your ways submit to Him and He will make your paths straight." (Prov. 3:5–6 NIV) Accept His instruction to move forward. Listen to Him with confidence, knowing that He is leading you in a good and healthy direction.

Your fellow journeyer,

Karen

Application:

> Have you come across a "Segway experience" in your own life? What might God be placing before you to try that you have yet to lean into? Make a list of the opportunities you have been given. Beside each of those listed, write down what may be holding you back from trying them. Pray that God takes that hesitancy and fear from you.

> Now make a list of new things you would like to try. Perhaps you do not feel that you have any opportunities. Then go make your own. Be adventurous. Pray that God gives you wisdom in what you choose and then learn to have fun with those choices.

CHAPTER 17

Fear Not

Dear One,

Fear. It is such a small word, but can create paralyzing emotions. Here are some powerful moments of fear in my life.

As a six-year old, I survived an F–5 tornado.

Moving when I was in third grade forced me to make all new friends.

Watching a horror movie as a teen caused me nightmares for years.

A trip through a blizzard during our young married years was terrifying.

Being told that I needed a cesarean section due to our first child being breech frightened me.

Facing the news that I had a lump in my breast and needed more testing a mere month after Alan passed away, was nearly more than I could handle.

I am sure you can make your own list of moments when your heart nearly beat so hard you felt your chest would burst. Life can definitely be scary. However, I have noticed that since Alan passed away, I am more easily upset. Smaller, everyday incidents tend to make me afraid.

Examples of fears I have experienced and conquered over the last three years include traveling and planning trips, making the major purchases of a refrigerator and a car, as well as learning how to pay the bills and do the monthly budget. With practice and the help of others, I managed to handle the scary challenges I was presented. I asked advice of an appliance repairman for a reliable refrigerator brand. My financial advisor accompanied me to the car dealership. Church friends taught me how to use budgeting software to aid in tracking my expenses.

While I have definitely made progress in handling these examples, one area in which I still struggle with is what the next ten years of my life will hold. After Alan first passed away, the thought of surviving the very next day terrified me. I can now look forward without dreading the next day. However, when I allow my thoughts to move too far forward into the future, I still find myself feeling nervous.

If you now find yourself afraid of things that would not have caused you any concern before your loss, realize that you are not alone. Feeling stranded without someone to help you is a common emotion and can certainly be frightening. Most of us appreciate knowing we have someone in whom we can turn to for advice and comfort.

How can you stop from being scared? Is there a way to be certain you are making wise choices for your future? Are people trying to take advantage of your current circumstances by rushing you through grief? Do you feel pressured to find quick resolutions without being given time to process and think things through thoroughly? When we are grieving, it is wise to not make big decisions alone. Realizing the wisdom in this practice, we can turn to the support of family and friends.

One of the verses I apply to my life reads, "Have I not commanded you? Be strong and courageous. Do not be afraid; do not be discouraged, for the Lord your God will be with you wherever you go." (Josh. 1:9 NIV) You may be thinking, "Right, easier said than done!" While that may seem true, it does not change the fact that God is with you. The "wherever you go" written in this Scripture, describes your journey through grief and all the decisions and frightening times included.

Your fellow journeyer,

Karen

Application:

> List those things that currently frighten you.
> Now write down why they frighten you. These fears may be hard to examine, but do your best. It will help make them less powerful if you understand the fear.
> Look at the positive side now. Make a list of your accomplishments, big and small. Seeing your success and

abilities can bolster your confidence that God truly is empowering you to heal and move forward. This is not the time to be modest. Rejoice in what God is allowing you to do and celebrate the victories.

➤ Now go back to your first list of fears. Pray over those items or activities asking God to also make you victorious over those. It might help to write those fears on note cards and then intentionally cut them into pieces. As you cut, determine that these are not things that matter to you. They no longer need to rule your life. Fear only holds power over you when you allow it to do so.

➤ Are there people that can come alongside you and help in the midst of your harder situations? If so, write down their names and plan to talk with them individually. If people hear how they can assist you, they are usually happy to help.

➤ Be sure to celebrate your victories and allow yourself to experience joy in seeing how far you have moved forward as you continue your journey. I am proud of you for facing your fears head on!

CHAPTER 18

An Unlikely Coexistence: Joy, Peace, and Pain

Dear One,

As I travel this journey of grief, I realize that I have missed some opportunities because of a false impression that there is a timetable to grief. I succumbed to the pressure of "waiting out" grief while denying myself the freedom to smile and enjoy life. How could I allow myself to laugh and take pleasure in things while missing Alan so much? Concern that people would not understand my actions and may think I was being disrespectful to Alan's memory held me back. I now believe I was wrong in accepting this lie.

No one has the power to tell us what we should and should not be feeling. While our friends may impart wisdom to us concerning our actions and choices, it is important that we are honest about how we feel and what we desire. There may be times when others need to come alongside to help us. As we walk through grief, we may not consistently be able to think straight and may become confused by our own feelings.

Though it may seem incongruent to laugh in the midst of grief, doing so can actually promote healing. Emotions tend to quickly and easily invade our days, causing us to cry one moment and laugh the next. This rollercoaster of emotions is common. Though the ride will be difficult, it will actually aid your journey if you allow it to run its course without fighting against it continuously.

Denying yourself the joy of a movie or laughing at a joke, thinking it unfair to your lost loved one, is not a sacrifice you need to make. I realize now that Alan would want me to smile, to have fun, and cherish life without him. It is okay. Embracing this lesson, I believe that conflicting emotions do coexist in our lives.

A perfect example of conflicting emotions occurred this past spring when our oldest son got married. What a lovely time of life – beginning a journey as husband and wife. The adventure of sharing new, young love and keeping house together is exciting and delightful. I remember my joy and excitement when Alan and I were wed nearly thirty years ago. I wanted that very same experience for my son and lovely daughter-to-be.

In the months approaching the joyous union, I had to face the fact that I was shopping and planning without my husband, feeling joy at the same time that I was experiencing sadness and sorrow. It definitely caused me to contemplate, reflect on my feelings, and determine how to move ahead. The last thing I wanted to do was put a damper on the upcoming celebration.

The morning of the wedding gave me just the opportunity to practice emotional coexistence. Austin, the groom, came to the hotel room early that morning. As I opened the door, he bounded in smiling and proclaiming, "I am getting married today!" I smiled saying, "I know!" Then, he, Chris, our younger son, and I proceeded to hug and cry together, mourning the fact that Alan was not there to experience such a blessed and joyous occasion.

We did not cry long, just a moment or two. However it was important that we allowed ourselves that time to acknowledge the loss before moving forward. Drying our eyes, I proclaimed that it was now time to make the day about joining two lives together. I wanted it to be a magnificent, happy day and we did just that! Moving forward without looking back, we jumped into the flurry of last minute preparations, photographers, limos, family, wedding vows, and honoring God.

I hope you understand what I am trying to explain. We did not put the wedding off and walk around moping or sobbing about our current situation. Neither did we ignore the fact that a key person in our family was missing. We allowed the opposing emotions to meet and then chose to move forward, heads held high, determined to make great memories of the day.

Have you faced such conflicting situations? When you do, remember to give yourself permission to feel and experience sorrow and joy together. Our lives are complicated. There is no reason to expect that our emotions throughout our grief journey would not be the same as well.

Your fellow journeyer,

Karen

Application:

> If you have experienced a similar emotional coexistence, journal about it. Rejoice if you were able to push through the confusing situation. Perhaps your event did not go as

smoothly as you desired. What can you improve upon to make the next opportunity better?

➢ If you have a special upcoming day – a wedding, birthday, or reunion – prepare your heart and mind for the conflicting emotions that may arise. Embrace the event and remember that making good memories will be something you can look back on years from now with a smile. Do not allow yourself to miss out on those special moments.

➢ Enlist people to pray as you approach your important days. Remember that you can do all things with Jesus Christ helping you.

CHAPTER 19

Questions

Dear One,

I have come to believe that questions are just part of life. Our society actually encourages young people to seek answers in school. It is good to be curious and take the initiative to learn. Having an inquisitive nature indicates you want to be educated and move forward. Realizing this, we should allow ourselves the privilege of inquiring about our current journey of grief and loss. While I believe some avenues of searching for answers are healthy, others are not.

"Why" is a question we may want to ask, but for which we rarely find a satisfactory answer.

Why did they get sick?

Why did they have to die?

Why am I in this situation?

Why did God allow this to happen?

Dear One, there are just some questions to which we may never know the answer and "why" is one of those. We can speculate and make ourselves miserable from asking this question. Our "why" will distract us and keep us from moving forward in grief.

In order to propel ourselves onward, we can instead turn that "why" question into one that is more constructive.

"What" is a great question to ask.

What do I do now?

What can I learn from this situation?

What should I do in this time of my life?

While the question of "what" is still very difficult, we can answer it most of the time if we are persistent and patient. Receiving help and guidance, either from people or from God, is not always instantaneous. It may take time. Upon receiving our "what" answer, a void is filled, a strategy can be formulated, and we are able to move forward in our grief journey. We are no longer helpless or hopeless in asking "what."

Another healthy question is "How."

How do I live like this?

How can I glorify God now?

How do I learn to find joy when life is so different?

When you are willing to sincerely ask "how," you can create a game plan, even if that is simply how you are going to make it through tomorrow or next week.

"Who" might be another positive question to pose.

Who has God placed in my life that is a supportive friend?

Who can I confide in?

Who do I know that is a good listener and someone I can trust?

Pray and seek to find this person among the already existing network of people in your life. Call your church pastor or a family member to help you. Be encouraged that as you find help and hope today, you will feel stronger. As you heal, you may eventually reach a point when you are ready to turn and help someone else.

Another great question you can ask in seeking help is "Where."

Where do I go from here?

Where do I find assistance and support?

Where can I find people going through a similar loss?

I have had wonderful, supportive people in my life from the beginning of my grief journey. Some of those people have moved away and are no longer in touch with me. Fortunately, I have made new friendships and connections that have filled those absences. My local Grief Share group has been invaluable in providing support of like-minded people going through a similar journey.

Whatever questions you may ask, know that your Heavenly Father hears all of them and cares about each one. We may not always receive an answer quickly, but there will always be an answer. Continue to wait and listen with patience and hope.

Your fellow journeyer,

Karen

Application:

> What questions have you asked on your grief journey? Are they healthy ones? Write out your questions so you can later record the answers, finding encouragement through them. Be aware that those solutions may look different than you expected. "For my thoughts are not your thoughts, neither are your ways my ways," declares

Karen Bransgrove

the Lord." (Isa. 55:8 NIV) Be open as you anticipate moving forward and watching your journey unfold.

➢ How can you reword your questions to be more positive and motivating? For example, instead of, "Why is this happening to me?" you might ask, "What can I learn from this?" I agree it is not always fun, but you will find yourself being more productive and feeling hopeful when the question is worded in a positive manner.

➢ Consider purchasing a new picture or poster for a room in your house to serve as a daily reminder that you still have hope and will find answers in spite of your loss. Better still, you may find satisfaction and enjoyment in painting one yourself!

CHAPTER 20

Treat Yourself

Dear One,

I had a wise friend who helped me see the importance of being nice to myself. There is nothing wrong with getting an occasional pedicure, taking a vacation, going for a long walk, or eating out once in a while. As long as those indulgences do not send you to the poor house, they are a great way to relieve stress and receive joy while you alter your usual routine.

At the beginning of my grief journey, I remember feeling that I did not deserve any fun or special indulgences. After all, a major change had just happened to my family and life was grim; therefore, I should be grim too. My reply to that statement now is a resounding "NO!" There are times when you will not be able to avoid feeling sad as you live through the hardship, pain, and sorrow of grief. In order to survive those difficult times, we need to embrace mourning and hold it close. In the midst of that turmoil, it is good to allow yourself some relief. Let yourself have some fun. Do not be afraid to smile and laugh. Your body, mind, and spirit require levity and relaxation in order to heal.

One of my very first indulgences was the purchase of a Kindle. I bought it ten months after Alan passed away as an early birthday gift to myself. It was something I had wanted and would use often. It has been the perfect treat that I have enjoyed immensely.

Another little present I occasionally buy is a special candle. The sweet aroma of baked cookies or pine trees wafting through the house allows me to relax and enjoy in the confines of my own home. The size and expense of my treat, whether being the Kindle or a small candle, does not dictate the amount of pleasure gained. Rather, it is the fact that I took time to care for myself.

Perhaps there is something you had always planned to do with your loved one, but did not have a chance to accomplish. Alan and I had talked about taking a cruise for our thirtieth anniversary. We never made it that far as he passed away during our 26th year together. While I seriously contemplated going on my own, I just could not bring myself to do so. Instead, I am planning my trip to Disneyland.

Setting a goal and planning ahead for a special treat will give you something to focus on while making it through each day. On my hard days, I like looking forward to fun activities. Everyone enjoys anticipating something special. While the upcoming trip to California will most certainly bring some tears, I am confident it will also be very good for me. Not only will it be a real treat to play on a new adventure, it will allow me a sense of accomplishment and healing as well. Plan away, Dear One. Part of the fun in a new adventure, can be the planning, preparation, and anticipation.

Your fellow journeyer,
Karen

Application:

> What gives you enjoyment? Is it reading a book and not feeling guilty about sitting for a few hours? Do you dream of getting a massage or pedicure? Perhaps taking a trip or buying a present for yourself is what you would enjoy. Write down a few ideas and begin mulling it around in your mind. Then make a plan to bring your desire to fruition.

> Knowing the items and activities that give you pleasure can be key to treating yourself. Thumb through some magazines or travel guides for ideas. Take the opportunity to create a wish book or dream board by cutting out those pictures to make a "Collage of Indulgences." As you are able to enjoy each of those activities or purchases, place a gold star on the picture to celebrate your progress.

CHAPTER 21

Here We Go Again

Dear One,

Tonight I received news that a friend's husband passed away this morning. Several weeks ago, they had been in a terrible accident while on vacation in another state. Upon both of them returning to Denver, she went home to recover from her injuries while he remained in a local hospital for treatment. His injuries were far more serious. He was healing and improving, the doctors optimistic that he would soon be released to convalesce at home. Therefore, his death was quite a shock and very unexpected. As I read the email this evening, I verbally gasped, placed my hand on my chest, and cried; weeping for the ache of my own painful memories as well as for that family now facing this unimaginable loss. I have walked the road of sudden death in finding my beloved gone with no warning. That initial shock is one I would never wish upon anyone.

How do we handle those times that trap us and cause us to once again unwillingly experience our own loss? How can we possibly be expected to continue to live through the memory of that trauma again and again? Reliving your loss at one time or another is almost a certainty as you find yourself bombarded with reminders on your grief journey. In fact, it has taken me several years to actually finish this book because going over my loss through writing has been a hard, long, painful process. Knowing that God does not waste anything in our lives, I believe we too, should look to use what life gives us for good purposes. Therefore, I have persevered and continued to write in order to convey what I have learned.

What exactly is that knowledge? A person experiencing a new loss does not know what to do. That person is, gratefully, functioning on autopilot, with grief acting as an anesthetic, numbing thoughts and actions. While the pain they are experiencing is deep, real, and excruciating, those of us who have walked that road realize it only gets worse in the upcoming weeks. Sometimes it takes months or even years for that numbness to wear off, allowing reality to ruthlessly appear and show its face.

Knowing a little of what the grieving person is experiencing, now what do we do with this knowledge? We can help them by prayerfully and gently guiding as they tumble into their own grief journey. Please remember that just because something helped us, does not automatically mean it will be helpful to others. However, we can definitely know what not to say. You may have experienced at one time or another those little words that scar and bite even though expressed by people meaning no harm.

Here are some condolences I was offered. While well-meaning people said these words, I did not find their statements helpful.

"God must have needed him in Heaven." ...God needs nothing. He is self-sustaining, and self-sufficient.

"You'll see him in Heaven." ...Yes, but I want to see him here and now.

"It is for the best." ...It does not feel like the best of anything. It hurts and I hate this situation.

"I bet you are ready to get things back to normal." ...Well, what is normal? I have to learn to live with a "new normal" and I do not care for it one bit.

By comparison, some of the most touching visits I received were from people who simply came to sit with me. These friends allowed me to cry and gave me the freedom to guide whatever conversation we had or did not have. There were no expectations placed upon me by their presence – I only felt acceptance, love, and support.

When we walk through grief, we do not always think clearly. Nor are we able to consistently accomplish necessary chores. It is often helpful for friends to come and do menial tasks around the house such as cooking meals, washing laundry, or doing the dishes. If the grieving person prefers to keep busy, then by all means, allow them to do so. They are not offended by your offer to help. Staying active may simply be a way of controlling one small thing in a world that has suddenly gone haywire.

If you ask the grieving person how you might help, you are likely to get no reply. I remember people asking me what they could do and I did not have a clue as to what I needed. I also was not always comfortable enough to ask anyone to go throw some clothes in the washer since that seemed like such an unimportant task. I did not want to hurt their feelings or be a bother. Being the center of attention and feeling as if everyone was staring at me was difficult at best. I was scared. My heart had not yet caught up with my head in realizing that God knew of my situation and was still in control. My world was chaotic.

Dear One, when you experience being thrown back to relive your grief, you will likely be emotional and exhausted. The pain, fear, and confusion you feel are very much alive and real. Absolute darkness once again rears its ugly head and attacks the progress you have made and the healing that has taken place.

Take heart, Dear One. Though the tears still course down my cheeks when my grief reappears, I have assurance. God has already taken me through this part of the journey once and He will continue to do so as many times as necessary. If walking through the pain periodically helps me stay authentic and in touch to better minister to others, then I accept that journey.

If given the choice, I never would have chosen this part of my life's path. However, that decision is not ours to make. God decides what occurs in life and has a purpose in our grief. He is not cruel nor does He decide to strike down people on a whim. Instead, He is a God whose plan and desire is to comfort us while bringing Him glory. He is the Creator. We are the created. He will always be more important, more knowledgeable, and more capable to handle what we cannot.

"To him who is able to keep you from stumbling and to present you before His glorious presence without fault and with great joy—to the only God our Savior be glory, majesty, power, and authority, through Jesus Christ our Lord, before all ages, now and forevermore! Amen." (Jude 1:24, 25 NIV)

Your fellow journeyer,

Karen

Application:

> ➤ Have you found yourself drawn into your grief again because of someone else's loss? If so, find comfort in recalling how God brought you through your original loss. Write down how He provided for you in the past and realize that His provision is still available to you today.

> ➤ Make a chart with two columns. On one side of the paper write a list of the things that helped you in your grief. Perhaps it was something someone said. Maybe you found a special Bible verse that really resonated with your heart on a particularly difficult day. In the other column, record the things that were not so helpful to you. The purpose of this is to not hold a grudge or plan a way to seek revenge. Rather, learn from your pain and the mistakes of others. Pray for wisdom as you encounter newly-grieving people. Strive to impart comfort and help instead of pain and confusion.

> ➤ If you are rejected the first time you offer help to a newly grieving friend, allow them some space. Do not be afraid to return and offer again in a week or two. As they process through their grief, the bereaved are better able to assess what they need and are more open to receiving help and assistance as it is offered.

CHAPTER 22

Placing Blame

Dear One,

Pointing the finger of blame is so easy.

"It is all your fault."

"If you had done something differently I would not be stuck like this."

"The driver of the other car was at fault."

"The doctor should have caught this earlier."

"God made this happen so He must hate me."

These are some statements that I have heard over the years as people have experienced the pain of loss. Blaming someone else for what happened to you might seem like the only thing you can do. Finding someone to be mad at or to hate may seem to make sense. However, Dear One, allow me to share with you why placing blame will only harm you in the long run. There are alternatives that are more helpful than holding others responsible for your loss.

We need to realize that sometimes there really is no one to blame. Accidents happen.

The choice we made seemed to be the right one at the time.

The tire blew on the car in the heat of summer.

The illness was found after it was too advanced to fight effectively.

There are just some things that we, as humans, cannot and will not ever know. The future is simply not ours to see. We could not have predicted that the tire would fail. The yearly check-ups showed no presence of illness. Placing blame does no good. Our loved one is not here to feel the regret you wish them to know, so why hold onto it?

When we place blame, we are focusing on what happened in the past instead of what is happening today and tomorrow. If we spend our time looking backward, how can we make wise choices to move forward? Being angry, bitter, and full of regret today only makes us ugly, vengeful people in the future. Happiness will not exist in the same heart as bitterness. They are rival emotions – they are opposites. In this instance, opposites do not attract. Instead, they tend to destroy and render us useless and unproductive.

God does not hate you. Bad things happen because we live in a sick and broken place. This is not what God intended for us when He created the world in the beginning. That was perfect and beautiful. Yet, because of man's choice to disobey God, sin entered and became part of where we live today. People get sick, poor decisions are made, and horrible things happen.

Take heart, Dear One, we do not have to be stuck in this imperfect world forever. Turn to the back of this book and read the chapter on "Meeting Jesus." Here you can discover how to live with God forever. It is possible to know beyond a shadow of a doubt that you will be part of a new world that will once again be perfect and beautiful.

Until we too are no longer living on earth, we must learn to live the life given us and we might as well choose to live it well. A great place to begin is without pointing the finger of blame. Realize that you cannot alter what happened. Accept that life is what it is and do your best to make the most of it. Do you really want to be bitter, angry, and unhappy?

Apply the tips and techniques in this chapter's Application in order to lessen your tendency to place blame. Equip yourself to accept your grief journey and proceed forward toward health and healing.

Your fellow journeyer,

Karen

Application:

> ➤ Are you blaming someone for your loss? If so, write down that person's name and the reason why you blame them.
>
> ➤ Next, be honest with yourself. Are they really guilty of an offense? If not, be aware the next time you try to place blame in their direction and choose to focus instead, on a positive attribute you see in them.
>
> ➤ If there is someone who has offended you, I encourage you to make the effort to forgive him or her. I realize this is not an easy request. Offering forgiveness requires time and effort. Ask yourself "Was it an accident? ...Did they truly intend harm?" Examine the verses in the back of this book on forgiveness and ask for God's help in beginning this process of forgiving and offering grace.

➢ It can be beneficial to get professional help if the blame and anger you feel is very deep and more than you can face. There are some wonderful counselors in this world who have the gift of listening and guiding people to see situations in a new and better light. Do not be afraid to seek counseling if you feel overwhelmed and unable to move forward in a healthy, healing relationship.

➢ Dear One, if you are blaming yourself for your loss, please know that God loves you and wants to free you from the pain and guilt of regret. On note cards, write down those things for which you are unnecessarily taking responsibility. After recording those items, take a marker and draw a line through them on your card, claiming that they are now God's concern. He alone is big enough to deal with them. Allow Him that task.

CHAPTER 23

Meeting Jesus

Dear One,

The Bible tells us, "In the beginning was the Word, and the Word was with God, and the Word was God. He was with God in the beginning." (John 1:1, 2 NIV)

Before the creation of the world, there was God the Father, God the Son, and God the Holy Spirit – the Holy Trinity, three in one. Each was involved with creating the world and creating you. I want you to meet God the Son, Jesus Christ, my Lord and Savior. He has been waiting your whole life for you to meet Him and is willing to do anything for you. In fact, He has already done the best thing for you anyone could ever do.

When God created the world, it was a perfect, beautiful place. Everything was amazing, all creation, (both animals and people), got along, and nothing bad ever happened. God made the earth and all that was on it in just six days and rested on the seventh, saying that everything was good.

His very best creation was people – Adam and Eve. The Bible tells us that God created them in Their own image – perfect. He appointed them to be in charge, telling them to name the animals and care for everything. Since the world was perfect, nothing ever went wrong or needed fixing. It was absolute paradise and was called The Garden of Eden.

When God made Adam and Eve, He did not want them to simply be puppets that could not think or do for themselves. He allowed them the ability to make choices. He then told them they could eat of anything, and enjoy the world made for them, with one exception. He forbade them to eat from the Tree of the Knowledge of Good and Evil, for if they disobeyed and ate of that tree, they would die.

Life went along for a short time, (the Bible does not say how long, but it was before Adam and Eve had children), when they were faced with a choice. The devil, Satan, disguised himself as a serpent and approached Eve, telling her she could indeed eat of the forbidden tree. If she did, she would not really die, but would just be like God.

Now think about this. Adam and Eve already had everything they would ever need – a beautiful world, plenty of food and water, continual conversation, and a relationship with God Himself. Yet, they both chose to believe the lie of the enemy and disobey God. Eve ate the fruit and offered it to Adam, who ate as well. When that occurred, the perfect world God had created was changed forever. Disobedience, or sin, entered. Upon that entrance, the perfection was lost and existed no more. Sickness, pain, evil, and death began.

Adam and Eve did not immediately die. However, God was truthful. He had warned that if they ate the forbidden fruit, there would be death. Their perfect bodies would no longer live forever as intended – and indeed, the aging process began. Worse than that, man was now separated from God. No longer did they get to walk and talk with Him. Instead, sin had placed an invisible wall, creating a barrier, separating man from God, which still exists today.

We read in the Bible, "all have sinned and fall short of the glory of God." (Rom. 3:23 NIV) No one is as good as God is. Sin is a debt now owed and requiring payment. Romans 6:23 states "the wages of sin is death." That sentence describes a separation from God forever. No Heaven, no happily ever after. Man is doomed. But wait! The second part of this verse is beautiful and full of hope and rescue. "The gift of God is eternal life through Jesus Christ our Lord." (Rom. 6:23 NIV)

God sets the standard of how to live by His own perfection. No matter how hard we try, none of us will ever be without sin. We have all sinned and failed. A perfect sacrifice was required to provide forgiveness for the sins of the world and pay the price much too impossible for man to pay himself. God, in His greatness, knew that man would need a Savior.

Realizing the predicament of man, Jesus Christ, lovingly and willingly came to our rescue. Jesus chose to leave Heaven, was born as a baby, and lived a perfect life on earth. Yet, He allowed men to sacrifice Him on a cross, dying for crimes He had never committed. Miraculously, He rose from the dead three days later, defeating sin and death forever. Dear One, Jesus did this because of His love and desire for each of us to spend eternity in Heaven.

No one can rid himself or herself of sin. We can stop doing things that are sinful, but that does not change the fact that we have already sinned. In fact, we are born sinners. "Surely I was sinful at birth, sinful from the time my mother conceived me." (Ps. 51:5 NIV)

How do we begin a journey and relationship with Jesus? How can we know for sure that we will spend forever with God in Heaven?

Steps to Jesus:

- Admit to God that you are a sinner. (Romans 3:23) Show regret for your sin by repenting, which means being sorry and making an "about face," to move in the opposite direction, away from your sin.
- Believe that Jesus Christ is God the Son, and that He not only died for you on the cross, but rose from the dead three days later, just as Scriptures foretold. We must trust and accept His ability to conquer sin and death. (Romans 5:8; Romans 6:23)
- Confess that you want Jesus Christ as your Lord and Savior. We must be willing to surrender our life to Jesus and let Him be in charge. Upon our submission, we learn to live for Him as the Holy Spirit takes up residence in our life. We will not be perfect, but because of the gift of forgiveness offered by Jesus, God will see us as a new, forgiven creation. (Romans 10:9; 2 Corinthians 5:17)

Dear One, remember that Jesus loves you. He died for you. Having a personal relationship with Him removes the invisible barrier caused by sin. His forgiveness is the only way to have peace on this earth and assurance of eternal life with God in Heaven one day. (John 3:16) When we surrender to Him, it is not that we lose everything. Instead, we gain everything through His forgiveness and we receive freedom from the penalty of sin.

If this is intriguing, you can pray and ask Jesus to be your Lord and Savior by following the steps written out above. I encourage you to find a Bible-teaching church and go ask questions to learn more. God wants to guide and direct through the Holy Spirit as you journey through your grief and discover the life He has for you. There are better days ahead, Dear One!

Scripture Resources

Verses on Forgiveness –

"This is my blood of the covenant, which is poured out for many for the forgiveness of sins." (Matt. 26:28 NIV)

"All the prophets testify about him that everyone who believes in him receives forgiveness of sins through his name." (Acts 10:43 NIV)

"Therefore, my friends, I want you to know that through Jesus the forgiveness of sins is proclaimed to you." (Acts 13:38 NIV)

"In him we have redemption through his blood, the forgiveness of sins, in accordance with the riches of God's grace." (Eph. 1:7)

"For if you forgive other people when they sin against you, your Heavenly Father will also forgive you." (Matt. 6:14 NIV)

Verses on Joy -

"I have told you this so that my joy may be in you and that your joy may be complete." (John 15:11 NIV)

"Very truly I tell you, you will weep and mourn while the world rejoices. You will grieve, but your grief will turn to joy." (John 16:20 NIV)

"So with you: Now is your time of grief, but I will see you again and you will rejoice, and no one will take away your joy." (John 16:22 NIV)

"You have made known to me the paths of life; you will fill me with joy in your presence." (Acts 2:28 NIV)

Resources

1   http://www.nlm.nih.gov/medlineplus/tears.html

2   www.griefshare.org

3   Alcorn, Randy. *Heaven*. Carol Stream, Illinois: Tyndale House Publishers, 2004.

4   Moore, Beth. *The Patriarchs*. Nashville, Tennessee: Life Way Press, 2005. Pg. 229.

5   Lemmel, Helen. Turn Your Eyes Upon Jesus. 1922. http://library.timelesstruths.org/music/Turn_Your_Eyes_upon_Jesus/

CPSIA information can be obtained at www.ICGtesting.com
Printed in the USA
LVOW10s0823310315

432626LV00002B/129/P